T0329202

POEMS

POEMS

BY

ALEC DE CANDOLE

CAMBRIDGE
AT THE UNIVERSITY PRESS
1920

CAMBRIDGE
UNIVERSITY PRESS

University Printing House, Cambridge CB2 8BS, United Kingdom

Cambridge University Press is part of the University of Cambridge.

It furthers the University's mission by disseminating knowledge in the pursuit of education, learning and research at the highest international levels of excellence.

www.cambridge.org
Information on this title: www.cambridge.org/9781107432949

© Cambridge University Press 1920

First published 1920
First paperback edition 2014

A catalogue record for this publication is available from the British Library

ISBN 978-1-107-43294-9 Paperback

BIOGRAPHICAL NOTE

THE writer of these Poems was born at Cheltenham on January 26, 1897. His first school-days were spent at St Faith's, Cambridge; in 1908 he went to St Andrew's, Southborough. Two years later he was elected to a Foundation Scholarship at Marlborough, adding to it a Senior Scholarship in 1912. At his schools he showed great promise and gained many prizes. In December 1915, he was elected to an open Classical Exhibition at Trinity College, Cambridge, his hope being to take Holy Orders in due course. In the following April he left school for the Army, and after training at a Cadet school in Oxford he received his Commission in the 4th Wilts. Regiment and proceeded to France in April 1917.

After short leave in the following September he returned to France, and was wounded on October 28, coming back to England in November. After some months on Salisbury Plain, he was attached to the Machine Gun

Corps, and went to Grantham in April. In July he left again for France, where he was killed on the night of September 3, 1918.

In March 1919, a small volume of his "Essays on Religion and Life," entitled *The Faith of a Subaltern*, which is now in its second impression, was issued by the Cambridge University Press.

The following pages contain a selection of his shorter poems, which have been printed in chronological order to show the development of his thought. He wrote, in addition, a Biblical drama, another drama entitled "The Fall of Carthage" and an "Arthurian Romance," in Spenserian stanzas. These, with the remaining poems, are excluded from this edition on account of their length.

A complete edition has been printed privately. Copies can be obtained on application to Messrs A. P. Dixon, Ltd., 9 Market Street, Cambridge.

H. L. C. DE C.

WESTMINSTER.
December, 1919.

CONTENTS

I

NOT once, but often, Truth has been rewarded
　　With fiercest hatred, foulest calumny,
While Vice has reigned supreme, by men belauded,
　　And punished all who would not bow the knee;—

Not once, but often, Truth with instant crying
　　Has called for champions till her champions came,
And then has giv'n them nought but tears and sighing,
　　A life of sorrow and a death of shame;—

Oft, having called on hero-souls to save her,
　　She seemed to grant them nothing but a frown;
Yet these have known her secret smile of favour,
　　A nobler guerdon than a kingly crown.

December, 1913.

II

O SLEEP, sweet sleep, come over me,
  And waft me to the land of dreams,
Where everywhere flow copious streams
Of honeyed wine, and every tree
Hangs down its branches to the ground
Fruit-laden, and on all sides round
The land smiles, beautiful and free.

No pain is there, nor any toil;
Far from the din of human life,
Far from the harsh unlovely strife,
Far from the tumult and the moil
Of struggling men,—there, far away,
In that sweet land the flowers of May
Spring aye unbidden from the soil.

O glorious land of dreams! I long
To visit thee and see thy bowers,
And lay myself amid thy flowers,
And spread my weary limbs among
Thy fragrant herbs, that so I may
Return to meet the toils of day
With manly heart, content and strong.

MARLBOROUGH, *Lent Term*, 1914.

1—2

III

TIME

O TIME, that fliest on never-failing wings,
Consuming years, consuming memory,
Consuming strength, and bringing vain regrets
For lost delight and ne'er-recurring hours,
Yet bringing with thee healing for the past,
Hope for the future, pardon, comfort, peace;
O kindly Time, thou canst not e'er return
To give us back the past, but thou canst give
Things better for the future; this is thine,
To soothe where thou hast wounded, and to dry
The tears that thou hast caused and at the last
To still life's tumult thou hast raised, in death.

MARLBOROUGH, *Lent Term*, 1914.

4

IV

O GOD, for Truth, or some faint glimpse of Truth,
 To smite through mists of night, and pierce the sense
And drive away the dreary vast offence
That 'wilders all the desperate heart of youth!
Mazes of life and death, of guilt and ruth,
 And all that binds the world in one intense
 Creative whole, that understanding dense
Can compass not, nor know a whit in sooth.
Yet grant us, wretched as we are, and weak,
 Grant to our earth-dimm'd spirit and fleshly mind
Even here, through this world, like some twilight-streak
 Of dawn, a vision of that which lies behind;
Or if Thou willest we must ever seek,
 Yet, ever seeking, may we ever find!

MARLBOROUGH, *November 21st, 1915.*

5

V

IN MEMORIAM

THIS life thus nobly ended, forth again
    Still to another!
Still God, through all thy future joy or pain,
    Be with thee, brother!

HASTINGS, *January*, 1916.

VI

—THE old, the bitter, everlasting Why,
That rises ever to the throne of God,
His human creatures' wail. And some have cursed
His name, as Fiend and Devil. Some have sworn
He is not. Some have said, "It is the LORD."—
Shall all things, at the end, be one, and good,
Or is it but the sport of careless Fates,
Or the blind workings of a hidden Chance?

    *   *   *   *   *   *

No; for a blow is God's own love, I think;
Not chastisement, but strength. The greater grief,
The greater love of God, the greater chance,
The greater strength. And God is with us still.

March 21st, 1916.

VII

AVALON

A WONDROUS isle is Avalon,
  Where grey mists cover all
The face of earth; and there, upon
  Their floating, rises tall
The shadow-shape of that sweet island, where
    There rest, in all delight,
    Past ages' fame and might,
Who now rejoicing hold that valley fair.

    There Arthur might we see,
    Noblest of Kings that are,
    And valiantest in war;
    With new-won chastity
Lancelot and Guinevere, those sinful lovers;
    And there is Merlin wise,
    All knowledge in his eyes;
And all the swimming mist o'ershades and covers.

8

And there our own sweet past
We might possess again,
Sweet-recollected pain,
And joy that could not last—
There, could we come there, there we still might dwell,
And love and laugh once more,
As we laughed and loved before,
And rest for ever 'neath the past's soft spell.

But onward is the call;
We must not, cannot, stay.
Still onward day by day
The future summons all—
Still onward thro' the heat and toil of the plain—
Yet, travelling on—who knows?—
Ere the endless day's long close,
Perchance we may find Avalon again!

CLIFTON, *June 9th*, 1916.

9

VIII

I HAVE not lived in vain, if one of men,
Who trod the earth and breathed the air with me,
Have felt the touch of man's divinity
From God through me, and learned to hope again.
And yet once more, I have not lived in vain
If, barren here, I have gathered into me
Seed that shall ripen in eternity,
Fruit to mature, and buds to blossom, then.
    Therefore I pray that God would fill my soul
    Full of the might and splendour of His grace,
    That I may journey toward Him not alone,
    But that full many another of His own
    May travel with me, and at last the whole
    Of all mankind may see revealed His face.

July, 1916.

IX

WEARINESS

TO all that's old and lovely and remote
From all the shock of facts we would were not,
Where pain and care and toil are clean forgotten,—
    Ay, all's forgot,—

Where we might fashion to our heart's desire
A world where all is happy, all is sweet,
Thither, in hours when all my heart is weary,
    Thither would I retreat.

Where souls may find the calm they still must crave,
Nor further toil, nor further strive nor stray,
Where hearts may find repose from sin and sorrow,
    For such a land we pray.

But yet no answer from the leaden sky
Comes down, nor voice, nor any that regard,
And so we struggle on, unstrength'd and weary,
Although the way is hard,

And strengthen'd so by pain and need's sharp spur
We tread the roughen'd path that all have trod,
Until we fall at length, content and fainting,
Before the throne of God.

OXFORD, *September 2nd*, 1916.

X

"THE truth of God is known,
    "Give up," some cry, "thy own
    Weak thought;
    Learn what thou ought,"

Is truth to some revealed,
From all the rest concealed,
    That so
    It may not grow?

And must we then seek God
By paths by others trod,
    And He
    Eternally

The same for us to know,
That knowledge now may grow
    No more
    For evermore?

What men knew once, must we
Unincreased endlessly
    The whole
    For every soul

Believe? But no such bound
Compasseth God around,
    The Light
    All-infinite.

Who filleth endless space
With majesty and grace,
    Doth man,
    With finite span,

All in full comprehend,—
That glory without end?
        Or say
    Is it that our clay

Can never hope to hold
More than we now are told
        Of Him,
    Whose darkness dim

Our eyes shall never pierce?
Oh! lay not such a curse
        On us,
    Who know that thus,

When we, (and thus alone,)
Shall know as we are known,
        Our earth
    Shall prove its worth

And life shall cease to seem
A loose and raving dream,
    And be
    Divinity.

Then trouble not, nor bind
The souls that seek to find,
    With chain
    Of the Past again.

Rising from what has been,
In ever-widening scene,
    May man
    Behold God's plan,

And still to hope and zeal,
May He Himself reveal,
    And each
    His wisdom teach,

That each, receiving so
What his own soul may know,
    May build
    God's Temple filled

By every spirit free,
That all for aye may see
    And own
    God better known.

October 3rd, 1916.

XI

WAR

WE never dreamed that war would come again,
That *we* should see men fight round windy Troy,
That we ourselves should feel the battle-joy,
That we should know ourselves the battle-pain.

We read of all the wounds and toil and heat,
Of noble acts, and mighty deeds of fame,
The building up of many a glorious name;
But, far away, 'twas bitterness grown sweet.

And now ourselves we plunge beneath its wave,
And feel the loss; and yet with purpose sure
All things, to save the world, we can endure:
—They save the world; themselves they cannot save.

But those who found thus nobly with their blood
A newer world, and those whose harder call
'Twill be to build it true, alike we all
Work in one hope and trust one boundless God.

November 4th, 1916.

XII

SUNSET

THE same sun sets, and spreads its colours due
 Broad on the evening sky, with gold, and grey,
Translucent crimson, and each perfect hue
That ever makes divine departing day,
As when to happier days it bade farewell,
Ere yet I left the hills and trod the plain,
But fresh and careless still I felt the spell,
Unhandselled almost yet of toil and pain.
And still it lifts me up from where I stray,
This vision of the loveliness of God,
This sight of coming or departing day,
Brightening with heav'n all earth's dull period.
And past, and future, and this setting sun,
In hope's clear light knit all my life in one.

ROMSEY, *November 8th*, 1916.

XIII

FRIENDSHIP

LIFE'S wheel runs back; and back Time rolls his page,
  That we may read where once we read before,
For one sweet day: the old wine, more rich with age,
For this brief space is ours to taste once more.
Dear God! how sweet it was, how sweet to taste
The joy of friendships old, yet ever new,
To pause, and there bid stand the years that haste,
So many as they pass, in all so few.
Grasp hands once more, let eyes meet loving eyes,
Ere to the future and the dark we go,
Then part; yet still, whatever fates arise,
We'll hope to meet again the souls we know.
Ay, somewhere—or the world's a lie indeed—
Our souls shall find the old friends, the old love, they need.

LONDON, *January 8th*, 1917.

XIV

THE soil of the land is holy,
　　Sacred to love and laughter,
But 't will only light the lowly,
Our skyey temple-rafter.
Others will deem the scene
Too desolate and dreary,
And hearts unschool'd and mean
Will find the worship weary.
But we will adore with tears
Earth below and sky above,
And anoint the perished years
With the unction of our love.

BOURNEMOUTH, *January 15th*, 1917.

XV

NIGHTFALL

(AN EVENING RIDE BETWEEN CORFE AND LULWORTH)

FROM day to night I rode, through evening chill;
 The rolling moors around gave summons keen
And called me on; and as the rainbow sheen
Of sunset faded, there, 'twixt hill and hill,
I touched the heart of Purbeck! Deeper still
Grew heaven's blue above me; shone serene
The kindly moon, benignant o'er the scene,
And God's sweet loneliness my soul did fill.
And as I rode, I felt a sweeping might,
For now the day was gone, the wind upblew,
The hills stood sharp against the sky's deep hue,
The trees were black 'gainst the moon's sovran light,
The rushing wind embraced me, and I knew
The wonder and the splendour of the night.

WAREHAM, *March 8th*, 1917.

XVI

A S one that stands upon the beetling sheer
Of some dread precipice, when midmost night
With whelming dark has hidden from his sight
The path before, behind him, far and near,
Nor knows he, blind, alone, what course to steer,
Yet still must on, though vast despair affright,
And wandering loneliness without the light,
The end so lost, the road unknown and drear;
So I, still following where my life did lead,
As on that hell-black peak have stood, to hear
And question fate; the future was a fear,
The past a phantom; yet for comfort's meed
Silence, no sound of wrath, no voice of cheer,
No strength save blind unalterable need.

Sutton Veny, *March 28th,* 1917.

XVII

TRANSLATION, HORACE c. ii. 14

"EHEU FUGACES"

ALACK, the years fly by to greet the past,
Nor all thy piety can hold the vast
Threatenings of wrinkled age, nor stay the hand
Of death inevitable that cometh fast.

Not thrice a hundred heifers slain each day
Could e'er avail to alter or allay
The unpitying wrath of Him who hath inbound
Geryon and Tityon with Cocytus grey.

And all who feed upon the earth and air
Must cross that river and must travel there,
Alike the peasant tiller of the ground
And monarch on his throne in purples rare.

In vain we shun the wars where blood runs free;
In vain the angry ragings of the sea
Tumultuous, we avoid; and all in vain
The hurtful breezes of the autumn flee.

For all must stand by that black river's flow,
And see the sluggish stream that winds below,
Behold the race of Danaus foul with shame,
And Sisyphus' long toil of endless woe.

Thy mansion thou must leave, thy wife adored,
While of the spreading trees that deck thy sward
So proudly, save the hated cypress none
Shall follow thee, so brief a space their lord.

Thy richest wine, beneath a hundred keys
Fast locked, and nobler than the cups that please
Kings at their feasts, thy heir, more blest than thou,
Shall drink, and tinge the pavement with the lees.

SUTTON VENY, *March 26th*, 1917.

XVIII

THE sunset clouds are glowing blue and red;
  Methinks they speak of past and future fate;
  For like blue hills behind I leave the state
I knew of old, and distant days now dead.
And crimson tells of days that lie ahead;
  For crimson are the hours that I await
  Of death, perchance, and pain and strife and hate,
And blood in darkness and in anguish shed.
And yet the blue still whispers of a love
  That led me hitherto, and evermore
  Will lead, through time and vast eternity;
  Therefore with GOD behind me and before,
Therefore with GOD around me and above,
  I yet may front the future hopefully.

In the train near ROUEN,
  April 28th, 1917.

XIX

THE wind that blustered yestermorn,
  And swept the ground and shook the treetops,
Then, howling, to the hills forlorn
  Passed on, and struck with rain their free tops,
Seems like a mock of Nature's mirth
  In scorn of man's strange piteous madness,
That shakes the heaven and scars the earth,
  And turns to horror all her gladness.
But when's at end this war of men,
  And all the world is at agreement,
Perhaps I'll stand and ponder then,
  And wonder what this wild weird dream meant.
Or from life's wilder dream again
  If first kind death shall gently wake me,
Or by his harsher angel Pain
  With fierce and cruel hand shall take me;

Still, when I've done with fleshly pain,
  And all the earth is left behind me,
Perchance I'll suffer yet again,
  And yet again may anguish find me.
Strange paths my soul must yet have trod,
  Strange sights beheld, around, above her;
Yet still in all is one same God,
  My Shield, my Stay, my King, my Lover.

FRANCE, *May*, 1917.

XX

LAUDABUNT ALII

L ET others tell of far away,
    Of peoples strange and cities gay,
Of mighty hills and rushing streams,
More fair than hope, more grand than dreams.
But England—give me England yet,
Land the heart can ne'er forget;
Where bounteous nature's riches all,
With man's to aid, are found in small,
As where wood and fernèd hill
Grace the gently flowing folds
Of slumberous Wye, whose bosom holds
All wealth of green by Tintern, till
A view majestic bursts upon
The sight to Chepstow, and 'tis gone,
Clear from the hills, to join its course
With rolling Severn, and the force

Of endless ocean, past the home
Of princely merchants, whence have come
Men who ventured lands unknown,
And threatening hills, and isles alone,
And over seas uncharted went,
And left enduring monument
In Canynge's soaring house of prayer,
And Temple's rounded pillars fair,
Of pious faith and love their own.
Southward thence my steps I turn
Where Mendip calls me, and I burn
To see once more the stretching plain
Beneath me, and behold again
The hill, where yet dead ages reign
By haunted Glaston—there the rest
Of Arthur and of Guinevere,
And Lancelot, of his knights the best;
Remains the spell. And now I go
O'er the old stone fences low
By Cheddar's cliffs, as yester year,

And by the lonely mines, and so
To where, 'neath Mendip's nestling breast,
I'll find the fairest and the best,
Methinks, of all the lovely west;
For there it crouches—ay, 'tis there,
Fragrant with beauty, safe from care
Beside the waters, ever-sweet
Beloved Wells! And there 'tis meet
Where saints have praised of old, I praise
The God who thus inspired to raise
These living arches' span, and mould
These breathing capitals of old,
And plan the Chapter's octave-sweep,
Here, in the place I love the best,
The home of sweetness and of rest.

Or may I awful silence keep
Amid the brown, mysterious waves
Of Purbeck's hills, where Lulworth laves
Its curvèd shores, and Corfe uprears
Its windy turrets, grey with years.

Or bid me seek the early flow
Of "stripling Thames," and happy go
Where swelling Cotswold hides his birth,
And loving hollows of the earth
Hold me alone from all but heaven.
Thence, by many a hidden town,
Where his silvery path is driven,
Down I'll go, and gently down
To Oxford city, home of peace
And patient learning's still increase,
Where Newman strove and Keble prayed,
And Morris, in that cloistered shade
Of Beauty, found it 'mid the past,
And toiled to make the world at last
Lovely, through work and beauty wed,
As once, he dreamed, in days long dead.
And on I'll go to Dorchester,
And bid adieu the river there,
And enter the long Church and pray
'Mid beauty of an earlier day.

So to those bare hills I come,
Whence I may view my final home.
I shall stand where runs the Horse
In ceaseless and unmoving course
By Uffington, and gaze around
On many leagues of smiling ground,
Bleak hills and leafy vale, as forth
I gaze on pasture to the north,
And Chiltern east and Cotswold west;
Yet from all the lovely rest
Southward with sudden joy I turn
To where I dimly can discern
The tufted trees that shade on high,
Distant against the clouds and sky,
The mighty head of Barbury!
And so to those dear lands I know
I'll go, as once I used to go,
By Liddington and hidden Snap

(Lost in the rolling downs' green lap),
By Poulton, or Four Miler's head,
Where I seem to grandly tread

Above the earth, or Savernake;
And so my joyful road I'll take
To happy Marlborough, name to wake
Sweet ghosts of memory, for the sake
Of pleasures gone, but dwelling yet
Secure where heart can ne'er forget!
There I'll go, and there I'll dwell
Amid the ever-happy spell
Of friendship's laughter, ever-new,
As in memory, firm and true.

So, in weak and faltering phrase,
Have I dreamed that I would praise
With loving heart the glorious land
Of England, where the generous hand
Of nature still has lavished free
All beauty, and has given me
To love it, wood and field and sea,
And flowing stream and barren hill,
Alive or dead, I'll love them still.

YPRES, *June 1st*, 1917.

34

XXI

CHANGEFUL with glow and chequered shade, a sight
   Now gloom'd with grief, and now with joy elate,
  How strange, how sweet, is life, how poised our state,
Now fair as day, now black as midmost night,
Well woofed with sorrow, webbed with strong delight,
   And love outlined above distrust and hate
    (Soul that with soul can conquer hell or fate),
Gladness that strives with gloom that strives with light.
And as we watch the shuttle to and fro
Weave out the pattern of our joy and woe,
   And bind the warp and weft's opposing strain,
We note the nobler unity, and know
By dark and light the beauty fuller so,
   And life more rich through joy's commingling pain.

RENINGHELST, *June 10th*, 1917.

35   3—2

XXII

FOR them, the bitterness of death is past;
  For us, we know not how our lot is cast,
To live or die, or worse, to suffer pain,
That rends and tears the body and soul atwain,
Until death come, a kindly friend, at last.

And stirrings deeper yet—I have loved the earth,
Known sorrow that enriched the after-mirth;
  The past was good, the future bright; I burn
  Still, still, to see the golden years return,
And plenty bear oblivion of our dearth.

But still, if hope, with each departing wing,
Should leave me starless, night-bound, sorrowing,
   Yet fate, my master, bids me follow still,
   Content, perchance: and if against my will,
I follow on, a bound and helpless thing.

Therefor I cling to hope: and yet my soul
Shall follow fate content whate'er the goal,
   So free, though every lightsome hope be gone,
   Can rest secure upon herself alone,
One small firm rock whatever surges roll.

June, 1917.

XXIII

IN that rough barn we knelt, and took and ate
Simply together there the bread divine,
The body of God made flesh, and drank in wine
His blood who died, to man self-dedicate.
And even while we knelt, a sound of hate
Burst sudden on us, as our shrieking line
Of guns flashed bursting death, a thunderous sign
Of raging evil in our human state.
Strange state! when good must use (nor other can)
The tools of ill, itself from ill to free,
And Christ must fight with Satan's armoury.
What strange and piteous contrast may we scan,
The shell that slays, and Christ upon the tree,
The love that died, and man that murders man!

PALACE CAMP, *near* DICKEBUSCH,
June 19*th*, 1917.

XXIV

ON A PICTURE IN ROME

("THE CRUCIFIXION," by Guido Reni, in S. Lorenzo
in Lucina).

AND so He died, alone. The eddying night
Of utmost dark that whelmed Him, when the cry
Exceeding bitter ascended up on high
Of one that dies abandoned of the light,
Seized on His spirit's fierce and desolate fight;
"Ah, why hast Thou forsaken me, oh why,
My God?" Despairing so He seemed to die;
Yet still His Church adores Him in the height.
Ev'n so. And we, too, by His grace, have known
The fierce and bitter joy of sacrifice
From Him, who at such all unmeasured price
Of blood and riving pain, to man hath shown
The love of God; therefore in all men's eyes
Was lifted up. And so He died, alone.

LA PANNE, NORD,
July, 1917.

39

XXV

THE breath of God, a wind from heaven's throne,
Like friendship's sweetness, and like pain's sharp strength,
Outstretching mightily to memory's length—
The free and wind-swept Marlborough Downs, my own.

Ah, Marlborough, Martinsell, and Granham Hill!
To see below the little town outspread,
Standing beside the old White Horse's head,
That "pads and pads," unmoved and silent still.

The twin grey towers, a double sentinel,
  The Chapel spire, the Mound, the Wilderness,
  The bridge, and Kennet's silver sluggishness,—
Ah, Marlborough, Granham Hill, and Martinsell!

To stand before the satyr-haunted wood,
  Or where I see the Vale beneath my feet;
  Beyond, the Plain's bare edges—ah, 'twere sweet
To stand again where often I have stood!

Or where I stand, up high above the earth
  On grand Four Miler's top, yet see beyond
  The waving trees by Barbury's ancient mound,
And share the wind's ecstatic solemn mirth.

Or where from Liddington I may behold
  The mighty plain that stretches out of sight
  Beyond dark Swindon town, and with delight
Gaze on a world, and wonder, as of old.

These are my friends: men, trees, and grassy downs,
  Deep starry nights, wide spaces, and the high
  Stern hills that teach our immortality,
And peaceful streams, and old forgotten towns.

These whom I loved, I honour and I hail,—
  All these,—because I do not know my fate,
  And yet I know my love so deep and great
That, death or life betide, it shall not fail.

August, 1917.

XXVI

ON A SONNET OF RUPERT BROOKE

"They say there's a high windless world and strange,
  Out of the wash of days and temporal tide,
  Where Faith and Good, Wisdom and Truth abide,
Aeterna corpora, subject to no change."
                                    RUPERT BROOKE.

THEY say: and yet to me the human gleam
  Of chequered life, and many-coloured love,
  Are nobler than the eternal things above,
Whereof sad weary mortals fondly dream.
The white eternity that must remain
  Calm 'mid creation's rack, unchanged in change,
  Less sweet, less bitter is, less nobly strange,
Than hectic joy, and love, and hate, and pain.

And he who fixed this wild and varied flush
Of infinite colour in human life, lest cold
Blank death should seize us, all shall re-unite,
We know not when nor how (as some great hush
May mingle many sounds), in one vast white,
Where yet each hue is shining as of old.

WAMBEKE, *October 3rd*, 1917.

XXVII

Ὧν οὐκ ἦν ἄξιος ὁ κόσμος

I SAW in dreams the mighty band of saints,
  Who lived on earth as men, endured and died,
Firm in the fight where fleshly nature faints
  Unmoved in faith of Him, the Crucified,
Who led them once through weariness and strife,
And leads them now in paths of endless life,
  Where they in rapture go their lovèd Lord beside.

And first of all that glorious company
  Is found the fair and tender Mother-Maid,
The Virgin blest to all eternity,
  Upon whose breast the Infant God was laid;
Next he, the leader of the Apostles' choir,
Who holds the keys; and he whose holy fire
  Spread first the gospel news, unwearied, unafraid.

And all the glorious Twelve, Christ's chosen friends,
　　And those great Four, who showed the Man of men,
The Lion of God, the slaughtered ox that spends
　　His blood for men; and he whose lofty ken
Saw things unspoken, things unspeakable,
In vision clear that mortals may not tell
　　Of Heaven's Throne, and God's high glory opened then.

And they who suffered torture, pain and death
　　By stone or rack or stake or wheel or sword,
Yet knew, like Stephen, 'mid their dying breath
　　The glory and the succour of their Lord,
And warrior saints who fought with Michael's strength,
And those who well endured a weary length
　　Of years, and died in His sweet peace whom they adored.

But who is this, the best and loveliest
  Of souls whom Jesus all in all sufficed?
And lo! upon his hands and on his breast
  And on his feet, he wears the wounds of Christ.
And after him he brings, like odours sweet
Before His Master, throngs whose willing feet
  By Francis' fragrant grace to Jesus were enticed.

The prophets' goodly fellowship are here;
  He who commanded, Let the people go,
God's chosen king, the psalmist and the seer,
  And fallen Ahab's still undaunted foe,
And chiefest he, who saw the holy Dove
Descend on Christ's baptizing from above
  And many a prophet more, whom earth shall never know.

And all who thirsted once for truth divine,
  Though dim, and held of good a love sincere,
See now the God they longed for, and they shine
  Bright in the glorious crowd rejoicing here;
Here Socrates and Plato find their goal,
And Virgil, and Lucretius' darkling soul
  Now lightened; sad Aurelius' doubts are now made clear.

And Dante holds the Paradise he knew;
  And they who, burning, raised a shining light
Of freedom, glowing yet unchecked and true,
  With great rejoicing worship day and night;
And Wesley's fiery zeal, and holy Ken,
And all of every farthest race of men,
  Who followed God, are here, in robes of glory dight.

And many millions more, to earth unknown,
  Who lived in Jesus, and in Him have died,
Who knows and stamps the flock of all His own
  With His own seals of love, are here beside,
And all adore Him still, and find in Him
Their guerdon, truth for eyes that once were dim
  Their God in Him, their King, their Pathway and their Guide.

He is their Rest, their Strength; in His great might
  They labour still on that eternal shore;
And working yet where never falls the night,
  One boundless God immortal souls adore;
And Him, their Lord, their Father, and their Friend,
Their Life, their Satisfaction, and their End,
  Cease not to praise, adore and love for evermore.

BAILLEUL, *All Hallows' Eve*, 1917.

XXVIII

IN MEMORIAM, J. N. E. (killed Dec. 6th, 1917)

A ND hast thou gone through gates of death?
    Though trembling nature bids us mourn,
    Yet passed from out this stormy bourn
At price of body and of breath,
Thou seest much we may not see,
    Thou knowest what we cannot know;
    Thus nigher God, through all our woe,
We deem thee, and our tears for thee
Are dried, who leftest earth as thou
    Didst leave us, brave in righteous strife;
    And all our memories of thy life,
Past joys and former laughter, now

We know not idle nor in vain,
But part of one tremendous whole,
The life eternal of thy soul,
And I shall speak with thee again,
And laugh, and know thee, and behold,
When I have passed, and, now unseen,
Thy presence is as it has been,
In friendship that grows never old.

MARLBOROUGH, *December 9th,* 1917

XXIX

ELEGY

WEEP ye for those who cannot come again!
   O weep for those whose sun is set in pain!
And let the rocks re-echo to our plaint,
The hills send back the voices of our mourning!
Lament and cry! nor know ye cold restraint,
But weep for those for whom is no returning,
Their sun already set, while still 'tis day;
And we endure a sad and partial light,
Reft of the radiant love that lit our way.
For death has left his toll of age, to prey
On lives unlived, and snatches from our sight
To silence those whom most we wished him spare;
And smitten hearts, first-struck with sudden grief,
Curse out on death, calling him cruel thief,

And eyeless fool, as one who in the green
Should reap the corn, nor wait the ripe and fair
Full crop of harvest-yellow;
Or pluck in June the hard and acid grape,
Nor wait the autumn richness of his shape,
Full-plumped, and sweet, and mellow;
But now he lies in wait to catch and snare
Lives unfulfilled, to whom the morn serene
Had promised deeds of fame, and high reward.
　　But these they have, and death's fell envious sword
Can sever not the honour from their name;
For these went forth, yielding their lives to death,
And therefore death is vanquished in their fall.
For now the doors of death are opened wide,
And we may gaze therethrough, and seeing, proclaim,
With bursting hope and yearning satisfied,
That that is true which seer and poet saith:
Their early promise is not crushed by fate,
Like some fair trampled bud that withers; dead,
They found their death a gate,

And passed from life to life; what did appal,
Now blesses, and their fear rememberèd
They smile at, and we guess their happy scene;
For Death in this his dread triumphal hour
Lays by his wonted guise of cruel power,
And lo! his form benignant and serene,
The All-Father's kindly angel; and the life
That struggled here, and yearned for mighty things,
Finds there as here the call to manly strife,
And as they were, they are, nor yet exempt
From human passions and from human love.
No sudden change is theirs, but on the wings
Of death upborne, they passed, and now attempt
With mightier weapons deeds our deeds above.
    Ay, and they help us also; greater might
Is theirs to aid in more than earthly fight;
And still their strength is ours, a sword and shield
Against the foes to which our souls would yield,
And still to earthly friends their love brings aid
When threat'ning ill makes flesh and spirit afraid.

For this, their home, where first they learned the spell
Of beauty, and the majesty of truth,
And such good things as now, though learning yet,
Behind a veil less dim than in their youth
Of bodily life, they see, ineffable
In glory—earth they still cannot forget,
Where many souls, to their soul strongly knit
With bonds of love unfading evermore,
Dwell yet, and love and holily worship it.
Be calm, and weep not; as they joyed before
In all the glories of the earth we adore,
So now in that enduring love they share
Of earthly friends and earthly beauties still.
For deathless love there is no power can kill,
And death no barrier makes twixt here and there.
And even we in flesh confined may yet
See heaven mirrored on earth, who dare behold
All things as one, and know the light eternal
Displayed in earthly glories manifold,
In every splendour of the round diurnal

Of tingèd dawn, bright noon, and lavish set
Of sun, attended as in regal state
By pomp of every hue that nature wears;
And then, till flushing morning comes again,
The awful glory of the silent stars,
Cold majesty, that weeps not for our pain,
Where all the passions of our love and hate,
Longing, and turbulent wrath, and aching grief,
Are melted into one eternal calm
Of moveless still relief,
Untouched by time and earthly things, and balm
Is found of fixèd peace;
And there, commingling in that waveless ocean,
Forgetful of desire and change and motion,
In those far burning depths all pulses cease.
    Ay, all the beauty, all the mingled dower
That life affords, and all the clouds which lour
That sun-rays doubly sweet may break therethrough,
All veils that half reveal the light beyond,
All torment giving place to sweet relief,

All strife and sweat by which our spirit grew,
All joy, all pain, all gladness and all grief,
And all the beatings of our human heart
Are theirs, and still they love us, and the bond
Of passion is not broken with the thread
Of bodily life, but each in his degree
(Those on the earthly and the heavenly verge
Of that grey flood we may not gaze across,)
Alike is an eternal precious part
Of one infinite human destiny.
And hence, though loud we mourn, and call them dead
Who pass, death is not loss;
But all in God and in each other merge,
Each single soul in one vast general soul,
Whereof no part is lost,
Or flung to mere destruction, like the frost
That vanishes before the noonday sun,
Or burning stars that earthwards darkling fall,
But even the vilest and the worst of all
Must still, through ages vast and numberless

Though 't be by suffering keen and long distress
Come purified and perfect to his goal,
And make complete the human race in one
Ever aspiring, still triumphant whole.
All we are one, nor long our severing,
And they with clearer eyes behold the earth,
And scan the heavens, in that glad rebirth;
And every generation following
Is one with us in everlasting worth,
Eternally doomed to endless perfecting.

December, 1917.

XXX

CHRISTMAS, 1917

TOGETHER we are glad and sing today,
Exulting in the birth of that sweet Child
Who to God's Father-heart has reconciled
Bewildered man, and lit with hope's pure ray,
And promise of endless life, his gloomy way;
Now sheltered calm, as in some halcyon mild
Retreat from war's black clouds and tempests wild,
This year together we adore and pray,
And if,—if, ere another Christmas dawn,
Death claims me hence, (as well he may, for plain
His path before me), yet my soul reborn
Shall visit you still bound in body's chain;
And after, met beyond, some joyous morn,
We shall share true Christmas mirth together again.

December 25th, 1917.

XXXI

SALISBURY CATHEDRAL

I PRAYED here when I faced the future first
  Of war and death, that GOD would grant me power
To serve Him truly, and through best and worst
  He would protect and guide me every hour.
And He has heard my prayer, and led me still
  Through purging war's grim wondrous revelation
Of fear and courage, death and life, until
  I kneel again in solemn adoration
Before Him here, and still black clouds before
  Threat as did those which now passed through are bright;
Therefore, with hope and prayer and praise, once more
  I worship Him, and ask that with His might
He still would lead, and I with utter faith
Follow, through life or sharpest pain or death.

December 27th, 1917.
  In the train near Salisbury.

XXXII

ENGLAND

[TWO SONNETS]

I

I CANNOT argue out the rights and wrongs,
  Who first this hideous force of war did move,
I only know my heart and spirit longs
  To serve this England somehow which I love.
Shall it be ours to dwell where England's hills
  Roll down in lonely places to the sea,
And hear the rushing waterfall that fills
  The vale with music's deep profundity,
And shall not love compel us, whatsoe'er
  This England asks, so beautiful, so great,
  Not hating, though the foeman merit hate,
But simply glad to pay, if need, the price
Of so much beauty in life's sacrifice?

II

Life thus, perchance, is short; but life is worth
  More, if your home is England; twenty years
Of living in the loveliest land on earth
  Are better than an age where Afric sears
The soul with summer's fires, or Arctic cold
  Numbs dead the very brain with wintry stress.
Yes, England, though thou listen to the bold
  And braggart cries of folly and shamelessness,
Flinging rewards to those who ask reward,
  Thy true sons love thee yet, and loathe the brood
Of cursèd traitors. Free thyself, and guard
  Thy noble heart unchanged, and ancient blood;
Thee will we answer, not the blatant breath
Of knaves, but thy high call, to life or death.

January, 1918.

XXXIII

HEREDITY

WHAT desires and powers are working in me
    Strains of long-forgotten ancestry,
Loves and hates, I know not, thoughts and passions
    Strangely mingled all, to furnish me.

Did some sire of mine in ages olden
    Yield an hour of passion now forgot?
I his offspring, lo! must watch and struggle
    'Gainst the lust that he regarded not.

Did he fight in chivalry and honour,
    Spurn his own life, spare a conquered foe?
Still that light beams on me as I wander,
    Shed from his fair deeds of long ago.

Yet, though thus the past surrounds and holds me,
    Strong in good, or baleful with its sin,
Forming me, and prompting yet my actions,
    Strange mysterious influence within,—

Still myself I rule within my spirit,
    Still I guide my purpose and my will,
Cherish yet my loves and aspirations,
    Persecute the evil in me still,

So to each succeeding generation
    Handing on the evil weaker yet,
All the good my fathers gave the stronger,
    Living on though all the world forget,

Lest my sons unborn should rise and curse me,
  Saying, "He, the recreant from the fray,
Now has cast a heavy weight upon us,
  His sin clogging our aspiring way."

Ay, for evil faints not in the battle,
  Still to war undaunted comes the right,
Each man's riven soul both field and warriors,
  Sharing all mankind's eternal fight.

LARKHILL, *January 22nd*, 1918.

XXXIV

HERE'S to the glory of life, to the good and the ill that
    we know
  To the loves and the passions of men as they move and they
    live,
To the hope of the future that beams, and the splendour of past
    long ago,
  All the chance and the change that the sweet-bitter seasons
    may give!

When I stand on the height of the hills in dominion, surveying
    the land,
  Where the ridges are silent, regarding the rivers below,
Then the course of their current I trace with my eye from the
    peak where I stand,
  Turning now to the towns in the plain, with their clamour of
    woe;

Even thus when I gaze with my soul for an hour on the surge
　　and the stream
　Of mankind, with its infinite ripple and chequer of change,
With its love and its hatred, its longing and laughter, its shade
　　and its gleam,
　Commingled of mirth and of care, and so heavenly strange,

With the pain that makes sweeter the pleasure, more happy
　　so desperately snatched
　From the sorrow that threatens the future, the ray the more
　　rare,
The more glowing, so caught through the cloudrift, the pang
　　of distress that is matched
　By the gladness enhanced, and the friendship the foe makes
　　more fair,

Then with wilder thanksgiving I praise the wise Maker of all,
    and adore
The Ordainer of sun and of shadow, the Giver of breath,
Life's fashioner, mingling the hope and the terror, behind and
    before,
Multitudinous laughter of life, and high promise of death.

LARKHILL, *January 23rd*, 1918.

XXXV

THE POETS

WE too can feel such pangs within our soul
　　As you can sing of; we too, we have known
The stirrings of such love, we can but groan
Within ourselves, nor utter, at the whole
Whirl of rich passions myriad-hued, that roll
　　Through pulsing human life. The winds far-blown,
　　The tossing ocean, grass and flower and stone,
Hill, valley, dawn, noon, sunset, fill the bowl
Of passionate love in hearts that overflow
　　In yearning silence, envying still your gift
　　God gave, to ease your souls in song, and lift
Strains that reveal your vision's fire and show
　　What we too see, yet cannot, all unswift
In speech, express, nor tell the things we know.

LARKHILL, *January* 23*rd*, 1918.
　　(*After reading " Gloucestershire Friends" by F. W. Harvey.*)

XXXVI

WE gaze upon the apple-flower in bud,
    Knowing decay will brown the pink-hued bloom;
We see a summer morning's sunshine-flood,
    Destined to meet the tempest and the gloom;
We mark the radiant course of youth's hot blood,
    Thinking how Death will chill it in the tomb:
And sadly ponder each, remembering
The winter that lies hid in every spring.

Yet from the frozen ground at last uprise
    The virgin snowdrops, pushing through the earth;
At last the sun breaks through the clouded skies,
    To fat the soil and chase December's dearth;
Even from the grave where man's poor body lies
    A fair and glorious hope restores our mirth;
And life and pleasure, flower and sunshine, show
The spring that lies beneath each winter's snow.

LARKHILL, *January 27th*, 1918.

XXXVII

THE BURIAL OF ARTHUR

THE night was dark on gentle Avalon,
   No moon reflected in the lightless mere
Remembered day; no beams of starlight shone
   With tender benediction; far and near
   The waste of waters spread, unbroken, drear,
Save for one only crest, a little hill
   That stood far-off, in grandeur black and sheer
In the wide lake that else the view did fill,
But could not top this peak, lonely, and calm, and still.

But blacker than the gloom of night, there came
　　Across the mere's smooth breast, a moving thing,
A boat, in silence and in hue the same
　　As those dark waters that it first did fling
　　So soundlessly aside, and after bring
Together, scarce a ripple showing where
　　The gliding ship had passed, which journeying
Carried them onward whom its bulk did bear,
And touched that lonely hill, and paused, and stranded there.

And three tall figures, vestured as the night,
　　Came from the boat, and stood upon the shore,
Beneath the silent mount's protecting height;
　　And as they came, with weary steps and sore
　　A coffin up the level beach they bore;
Far had they come, and far from field and town
　　Had brought their burden; now they came, once more,
Under the cover of Night's darkest frown,
At their long journey's end, weeping, to lay it down.

For hither from the shores of Lyonnesse
They voyaged, and the gaze of Bedivere,
The last of Arthur's knights whom that distress
Had left, that slew in one dark day of fear
His Table Round, and all his followers dear,
Comrades in many a battle's fierce delights;
Now all are gone, three queens have brought him here,
Him, the slain victor of a hundred fights,
Arthur, the flower of kings, the noblest knight of knights.

And as they bore him slow, uprose the moon,
Touching with darts of light the watery ways
In twinkling silence, calm and sweet; and soon
O'er those sad forms she shot her silver rays,
Whereat the mourners paused a little space,
While newborn hope seemed first their hearts opprest
To melt to peace, as full on Arthur's face
The moonbeams fell, and where upon his breast
His hands were crossed, as there he lay in kingly rest.

So standing there, they prayed a little while
　For Arthur, and the land he left forlorn,
And still the moon-rays seemed like Heaven's smile
　In answering blessing, promising the morn
　Should follow darkness, and the realm so torn
Be healed; and then again they moved, and found
　A new-dug grave, where him whom they had borne,
Full reverently, with no profaning sound,
They gave to peace at last, and laid within the ground.

And there they knelt, and each one with her veil
　Covered her face in mourning and in prayer,
Yet none, for all their sorrow, with a wail
　Profaned the dim and deathly silence there;
　But when they rose, the moonlight soft and fair
Showed them a form majestic, solemn, old,
　Robed all in white, but his grey head was bare;
They gazed in awe, such aspect to behold,—
And, "Who art thou?" said one, whom wonder had made bold.

"Lo, I am he," he said, "who first foreknew
The reign of Arthur; from the raging sea
I took him; while he then to manhood grew
Strength, wisdom, valour, first he learned of me;
Know ye not Merlin? I who bade him free
The realm of heathen foes, and by my spell
Brought him Excalibur, lo! now that he
Is fallen where his knights around him fell,
I come to bring you hope, and future fame foretell,

"Arthur shall sleep in gentle Avalon,
And time and solitary sleep shall heal
His grievous wound, and he shall slumber on,
Not dead indeed, for still, unmoved and leal,
Within her heart this mighty realm shall feel
His spirit stirring, and his living power
And dauntless valour still her soul shall steel;
And when the storm-clouds deepest o'er her lour
Arthur shall come again, to aid her darkest hour.

"So leave him, queenly mourners, who have borne
    His body hither, leave him to his rest;
Here in this vale, through many a night and morn,
    He shall be soothed upon the earth's kind breast,
    And after so long war, with peace be blest
Long time; yet still his spirit her watch shall keep,
    Though here his flesh repose; and if, opprest,
His country call him, howsoe'er to sleep
He seem, her cry shall rouse him from his slumbers deep.

"But go ye hence, and wait that glorious day."
    And so the three mysterious queens arose,
And o'er the moonlit waters sailed away.
    And Merlin that strange way the wisest goes
    No long time after went; and he who knows
Can show where hills remote that gently rise
    Shut in a valley where the river flows,
Beside whose stream, 'mid trees, and birds' wild cries,
Beneath an ancient mound the mighty Merlin lies.

But still they tell that tale of ancient time,
  The happy years of Arthur's golden reign,
And still they speak of Merlin's wizard rhyme,
  And long for Arthur to return again;
  And o'er his tomb they built a glorious fane,
And worshipped God that sacred grave upon;
  And 'mid green fields the ruins still remain,
Where men may stand, and muse on Arthur gone,
There in the misty vale of gentle Avalon.

LARKHILL, *February*, 1918.

XXXVIII

PROFICISCENTI

I

NOW God be with you wheresoe'er you go;
 God knows I would that I could go instead;
My little worthless life—dear friend, you know
 How little loss it were if I were dead.
But you tune songs such as I fain would sing,
 You have dared such things as would that I could do;
In music, action, suffering, everything,
 My sum is still a moiety of you.
Go, since you must, those strange and fearful ways,
 Where death screams loud in hurtling of a shell;
Would I might too!—But though my body stays,
 My spirit goes with you to the heart of hell.
For souls once stamped with love's immortal brand
Eternally inseparable stand.

Full merrily you went; yet my heart yearned
 That you should go from England once again,
To tread the paths of death and danger spurned,
 The darkling troublous ways of fear and pain.
Happier I was myself to go away;
 For then the man that went, perchance to die,
By life and death's grim borderland to stray,
 Was not a friend of mine, but merely I.
Call me not fool or braggart, if I know
 That love awaked, in ev'n so poor a heart
As mine, desires and pants and suffers so,
 To serve what is of its own self a part;
Nor even death can sever loves so sweet;
If not on earth, beyond it, we shall meet.

March 1st, 1918.

XXXIX

LINCOLN MINSTER

I CANNOT voice thy glories; all too cold
  Is human speech to tell of human art,
   That strikes, like Lincoln, to the inmost heart
With tender touch of loveliness untold.
What work is here! Not labour bought and sold,
  But love that bursts to life in every part,
   In stem and foliage, flower and fruit, that start
From the quick stone. O toil unpriced of gold,
O built for ever, sharing sacred days
  Of story rich with many a saintly name,
   Still may'st thou flourish with no weaker fame,
That ever thou on high may'st proudly raise
  Thy towers on Lindum hill, that thee proclaim
Wholly supreme and royal, passing praise.

May 11th, 1918.

XL

UTI CONVIVA SATUR

NOW, if I die, so be it. I have seen
    The towers of Lincoln soaring from the hill;
  Passed the broad breast of Mendip, to the still
Sweet spot where Wells sits thronèd as a queen;
Beheld in Glastonbury what things have been
    In golden ages past; and felt the thrill
    Of eve in Purbeck, gazing rapt until
On sea and shore night dropped her darkening screen.
But best, I have exulted as I went
    From Marlborough o'er the ancient downlands bare,
    To Totterdown or Hackpen, or to where
Free Barbury lifts a head by storms unbent:
    I have had earth's blessing full and rich and fair,
  And if I die, I well may go content.

May 27th, 1918.

XLI

IN CRUCE REGNANS

ENTHRONED above the sages and the saints,
   Above all kings that e'er had empery,
   And wielded sceptres over land and sea,
More nobly crown'd than all that fancy paints
Of any monarch,—lo! thy life-blood taints
   Thy cross of unimagined agony,
   Whereon, thorn-diadem'd, thus patiently
Thou hangest, while to death thy body faints;
Therefore thy crown is every crown above,
   Thou mighty martyr of the truth divine
   Declared for ever in the cross thy sign,
The ultimate teaching thou dost seal and prove
   In that unfathomable death of thine,
The highest good, self-sacrificing love.

June 30*th*, 1918

XLII

A S one who wanders on a desert plain,
An arid waste of dead sterility,
Then finds a green oasis suddenly,
And slakes his thirst there, and forgets his pain,
Resting awhile from the long journey's strain
'Neath the cool shade of some o'erarching tree
In full content, and yearneth longingly
In that sweet place for ever to remain;
So has it been my fortune all this day
Beneath the cloud-flecked blue of heaven's wide dome
To rest in quiet ease, my spirit at home,
All weary care and labour put away,
Free now and happy, ere again I roam,
Once more in void and barren paths to stray.

July 7th, 1918.

XLIII

A ND if a bullet in the midst of strife
Should still the pulse of this unquiet life
'Twere well: be death an everlasting rest,
I oft could yearn for it, by cares opprest;
And be 't a night that brings another day,
I still could go rejoicing on my way,
Desiring in no phantom heav'n to dwell,
Nor scared with terror of any phantom hell,
But gazing now I find not death a curse
Better than life perchance, at least not worse;
Only the fierce and rending agony,
The torment of the flesh about to die,
Affrights my soul; but that shall pass anon,
And death's repose or strife be found, that gone;
Only with that last earthly ill to cope
God grant me strength, and I go forth with hope.

July 17th, 1918.

XLIV

H AST thou beheld a night of burning stars?
　　With ev'n such silent eyes does GOD behold
　The world and all its sorrows from of old,
The pangs that torture, and the strife that jars,
The abounding evil that infects and mars
　　The glories of our being manifold.
　Hast thou not cursed those eyes of splendid gold,
That pity not our sufferings and our wars?
But who can tell the love deep-hidden there,
　　Or doubt that gladsome day shall follow dark?
　And as we know the sun's rekindled spark
Shall flood the earth again with radiance fair,
　　So may the silent Power that seems so stark
At last for man some glorious dawn prepare.

August 4th, 1918.

XLV

WHEN the last long trek is over,
 And the last long trench filled in,
I'll take a boat to Dover,
 Away from all the din;
I'll take a trip to Mendip,
 I'll see the Wiltshire downs,
And all my soul I'll then dip
 In peace no trouble drowns.

Away from noise of battle,
 Away from bombs and shells,
I'll lie where browse the cattle,
 Or pluck the purple bells;
I'll lie among the heather,
 And watch the distant plain,
Through all the summer weather,
 Nor go to fight again.

September 2nd, 1918.

Printed in the United States
By Bookmasters